From Here to THERE

From Here to THERE
A Tale of Love

By Elsita Sterling

SterlingPress

Maui, Hawaii

From Here to THERE, A Tale of Love

Published by
Sterling Press
535 Kupulau Drive
Kihei, Hawaii 96753 USA
www.ministryoffun.com
Additional copies may be ordered through the website
or by email to books@ministryoffun.com

Cover design by Ann Wilson Taylor
of *gel e fish graf x*, Maui, Hawaii
annie@zenamaestro.com

Interior design by
Charlotte Thomson and Ann Wilson Taylor

Production by *gel e fish graf x*
Post Office Box 359, Kihei, Hawaii 96753

Printed in the United States of America
by Lightning Source, Inc.

Library of Congress Card Number: 00-192709
ISBN Number: 0-9706294-0-0

I dedicate this book of poetry to
the Dawn of Peace in every heart,
in this, our new millennium.

E. S.

Acknowledgements

I am deeply grateful to Charlotte Thomson for her friendship, patience, and skill in artistically organizing these poems into manuscript form.

Thanks go to Ann Wilson Taylor, who created a radiant cover design inspired by my small sketch of "The Sun of Life". Ann guided the book production through publication, and also designed the www.ministryoffun.com website which includes the Sterling Press pages.

Finally, I offer my heartfelt appreciation and love to Valerie Ward, whom I call "Invaluable Val", for her kindness, companionship and help in countless ways.

Table of Contents

BEFORE

BEFORE (continued)

DURING

SINCE

SINCE (continued)

SINCE (continued)

Introduction

Duncan Sterling, Jr. and I were neighbors and good friends for many years, and our children grew up together. We were married, both widowed, when I was eighty-three and he was eighty-two. We had three lyrically happy years together before he was felled by a stroke.

My daughter, LiLi Townsend, flew from the Hawaiian Islands to be with us during these difficult times. She drove me to the hospital each day. Duncan could not speak and could barely move. I wrote poems, some sad, some hopeful. The hospital nurses, who were so kind to me, urged me to publish the poems. "Hundreds—no, thousands of people all over the world are feeling the same anguish that you are: seeing a loved one lying out of touch with all that he had ever known before. But you have the gift of words! These poems could help to ease so much pain."

Six months later, at three o'clock in the morning, with LiLi and me beside him, Duncan's spirit departed for the next world…

Some time later, I collected the poems I had written during this painful time and found that there were only twelve—hardly enough to make a book! So, I combined them with others I had written over the years, dividing them into three parts and naming them BEFORE, DURING and SINCE. That these poems bring pleasure and some comfort to others is my dearest wish.

E. S.
September, 2000

BEFORE

Memories

How can a precious memory be captured,
Held fast against the wily thief called Time?
Words can do it, if you find the right ones
To seal it in the crystal of a rhyme.

Happy New Year!

When first your lips met mine,
In a Happy New Year's kiss,
My soul stirred in surprised delight —
"Hello!" And, ever since,
We cannot bear to be apart, for long.

Recognition

I did not know
It was Love that I felt;
I thought it was just admiration.
I did not recognize Love —
But Love recognized me.

The world receded
Into the distance,
And there was only You.

Lasso

I roped you in with the kiss of a friend;
That's all it was meant to be.
But we both were caught in the Noose of Love,
Which will not set us free.
For the Noose of Love is a Noose of Light
Which encircles you and me.

It's You!

"It's You! It's You!" my heart sang with joy
As Love opened the door.
"It's You! It's You! It was always You!
But I didn't know it before."

Star Sapphires

His eyes are like star sapphires,
Mysterious and beautiful.
Through them, I have glimpsed
The strong and gentle soul within.
I see the love and tenderness
But the eyes are impenetrable,
And the soul retains its secrets
Even from himself.
Who are you, my love?
But then, who am I?
Some day we will know.

When You Are Away

I miss
The tone of your voice
When you're saying my name,
The smile on your face
When we're playing a game,
The light in my heart
When you kindle the flame.
I miss you when you are away.

I miss
The glow in your eyes
As they gaze into mine,
The lift in your kiss
Like a very fine wine,
The clasp of your fingers
With mine intertwined.
I miss you when you are away.

Summertime

Blooming cosmos bend
'Neath laden bumblebees
And the fragrance of the roses
Is borne upon the breeze.

Adventures with LiLi

Prayer of the Lunar Eclipse in Egypt
Tropical Interlude
Dolphins
Three Witches from Out-of-Town
To LiLi

Prayer of the Lunar Eclipse in Egypt

I leaned my back against the sun-warmed obelisk, as I sat on the stone at its base, and my heart was filled with wonder and gratitude. I wished I could offer something in appreciation of all I had received, and the thought came, "Make a prayer for our planet."

That night there was a partial eclipse of the moon. We joined a group of friends and seekers in the beautiful Temple of Karnak and, in a moment of silence, I prayed aloud:

"Oh Mother-Father God,

In this moment of awesome beauty, we pray for our planet, which we love but which, in our ignorance, we have so badly treated.

Please help us to restore its purity and integrity so that its waters, from which we rose, may again sparkle like crystal, its oceans, lakes and rivers may flow in clarity and the fishes, whales and dolphins that inhabit them may rejoice.

Help us to purify the air over our heads and the earth under our feet, so that the planet may be green and wholesome and the woods and jungles flourish, so that the birds of the sky and the beasts of the field may again be healthy and the creatures of the forests find shelter and multiply.

Above all, may the hearts of men be purified, so that misunderstandings that have divided them may disappear and the Most Great Peace come to pass."

And as we prayed, Earth's shadow, which had darkened the face of the moon, moved away and she was revealed in all her glory.

Tropical Interlude

*A visit with my daughter, LiLi,
to the beautiful French island
of St. Barthélémy
in the Caribbean Sea*

Le Camp

There is no television at Le Camp,
No radio, no telephone, no fridge,
No ice, no running water, hot or cold.
There are no doors, no windowpanes, no keys.
There is the mighty ocean, sapphire blue.
There are the trade winds, drifting gently by;
Bougainvillea, purple, flame and pink,
Scarlet hibiscus and plumbago's fairest blue,
Coco palms and mangoes, hummingbirds
And little lizards leaving rope-like trails
In the soft sand. There is the sun,
At night, a million stars, the moon —
It's Paradise!

Grignotte

A little cat of wistful mien,
With pointed ears and eyes of green,
Companion of our sleeping hours,
A tiny tiger in the flowers.

Sailboat Race Around the Island

The sea is blue and the sun is bright.
The world is bathed in golden light.
And — I miss you.

The ship is trim and the crew is stout.
The wind blows strong as we come about.
The great sails fill, my heart stands still.
And — I miss you.

Aquarium in a Small Café

Crustaceans weave a stately dance,
With rhythmic tread and pointing lance,
Within a measured jousting place,
Closed *cuirasse* and visored face,
And, just when War seems beyond doubt,
Forget what it is all about.

All That I Lack in Paradise

Only your voice to tell me you love me,
Only your arms to hold me tight,
Only your lips to bring enchantment,
Only your presence through the night.

Underwater Fantasy

Tiny fishes swirling in a vortex,
Seaweed swaying to a silent tune,
Monsters lurking in their murky caverns,
Dolphins playing in the light of the moon.

Loneliness

The constellations have a different shape.
The rustling palms are foreign to my ear.
I can't forget the sweetness of your love.
And, even though I try,
I can't recall the contours of your face.

The Lizard

A lizard's black unblinking eye
Will catch the flicker of a fly.
And lightning quick,
Its supple tongue
Will snatch it
On a hill of dung.

While Back in Bayville...

As you sit among the flowers
In your quiet orchid bower
And your thoughts are often wandering
To me,
I am lying by the ocean
In a veil of suntan lotion
And I wish that you were lying here
With me.

The Last Day

A feast was laid
In the dappled shade
Of the round-leafed sea-grape tree;
Chicken and pâté,
Wine and bread
Under the spreading
Branches spread
While the sun shone bright on the sea.

Small waves danced
On the broad expanse
Of the sweetly-curving bay
Where a heady brew
Of jade and blue,
Turquoise and lilac
And unknown hue
Entreated us to stay.

So, one more swim
In the sparkling sea
And one more bask in the sun,
Just one more stroll
On the silken sand
And the last day will be done.

Now the sun is low
And a copper glow
Is spreading on sea and shore.
Our voices still
As we climb the hill
Til we see the cove no more.

Soon the moon will rise
In the darkening skies
And the constellations blaze,
And the golden day
Will have gone its way
With all the golden days.

Dolphins

How would you feel if you wandered alone in the rough, sandy hills of Montana and a wild horse eyed you from afar? Suppose that he tentatively approached, delicate nostrils aflare for a scent of danger, sensitive ears alert for a threatening sound. Suppose that he minced forward, step by step on his small hooves and laid his velvet muzzle in your hand. How would you feel?

Suppose that you stood alone on a lofty hill and perceived a distant speck in the sky. Suppose that it circled in majestic sweeps and suddenly you realized it was an eagle. Suppose that his circles narrowed and he descended until close enough for his icy eye and the subtle markings of his feathers to be seen. Suppose that with a rush of air from his mighty wings, he alighted on your outstretched arm. How would you feel?

Suppose that you walked alone and without fear in the teeming jungle and stopped to rest under a tree. As you leaned your back against its trunk and the silence again became alive with jungle sounds, suppose that you saw among the streaked shadows, some different streaks, and then you saw two golden eyes. Suppose that they looked at you without ferocity and that the great beast arose and emerged from the protecting foliage and you could see the black and orange stripes and the powerful muscles rippling under his skin. Suppose that he approached and, with a sigh, he lay down beside you and you passed a hand over his silken hide. How would you feel?

It is all these things when you are close to the dolphins, but more, much more. They are a law unto themselves and hold a secret which they are tantalizingly keeping — just out of reach. They have dwelt upon this earth long before the appearance of man. In spite of the way we have treated them, they love us and like to be close by, but we have never even tried to understand them, until now.

The dolphins keep their secrets
But their message is clear:
Love brings Trust.
Trust banishes Fear.

Three Witches from Out-of-Town

Three wise witches from Out-of-Town
Flew in one night last week,
With tinkling bells and potent spells,
A newborn babe to seek.
Their radar and their sonar
Pointed just one way,
To Houseboat Row, not far to go,
Just South, across the bay.
There, in a wicker cradle,
The precious babe they found,
In a gently rocking houseboat,
With one foot on the ground.
"Oh, what a perfect landing place
For such a special one,
Where she can watch the rising moon
And the setting of the sun;
Where she can hear the rushing wind
And the seabirds' lonely cry
And the honking of the wild geese
As they streak across the sky."

The witches smiled and tinkled their bells
(Too soft a sound to hear)
And said, "Mikaela Elizabeth,
Listen and be of good cheer.
For we have brought you presents,
Gifts from far away,
To brighten your eyes and gladden your heart
And help you on your way.
We are your three fairy godmothers
And these are the gifts we bring:
A clear mind and a true heart
And a voice to speak and sing
And tell of the wonders forgotten
And the wonders yet to be,
If people will only remember
That it's Love that sets you free."

To LiLi

The hours of life are like a necklace,
Beads of gold and green and blue,
Somber grays, and some black onyx,
Pink tourmaline the hours with you.

Back Home

There's a feeling of Spring in the air.
There is nothing to see yet,
Nothing to hear yet,
Really, nothing at all but a feeling.
I think it must be a feeling of Spring
In my heart.

Separation

When you left me,
I stood still in my tracks,
Awaiting the signal to **GO**!
For life had lost its luster.
The river was blocked
And unable to flow.

When you returned to me,
Barriers opened.
The River of Life
Flowed again.
The sun shone, the birds
Started singing —
My world was
In order again.

The Strongest Heart

The heart that is mended
By the one who broke it
Is the strongest heart of all.
It is melded by molten gold.

Duncan and I were married in 1988 when I was eighty-three and he was eighty-two. He teased me by calling me a "cradle snatcher" for marrying such a young man! The following twenty-four poems were written during our short and happy marriage.

On Our Wedding Day

Tomorrow becomes Today
As Time opens the door.
Today will soon be Yesterday
But Tomorrow is *Evermore*!

Sterling Is Silver

I love the name that you gave me
And am happy to call it my own, for
Sterling is silver,
Sterling is true,
Sterling's enduring
As is my love for you.

This poem came to me in a dream, where I attempted to recall which of Shakespeare's plays the sentiment was from. When I later realized it was not from Shakespeare at all, I decided that even though Juliet never said it to Romeo, Elsie could certainly say it to Duncan!

January 1, 1989

A CARD CELEBRATING OUR FIRST NEW YEAR TOGETHER AS HUSBAND AND WIFE

One Home,
One January,
One Life,
One Love,
One You!

Happy, Happy New Year!

Man and Woman

Oh, the bigness and the smallness,
The hardness and the softness,
The straightness and the roundness
That make up You and Me!

My Choice

My spirit has chosen
To be here with you.
My spirit has chosen
To you to be true.
With you, my beloved,
I've chosen to be
Throughout this life
And through Eternity.

We Are Two

We are two,
Me and You.
To be but one
Would be no fun!
We must adjust
Til You and Me
Are We.

Opening of the
Wild Turkey-Shooting Season

These little separations
Are very sweet, my love.
They let us know
That, when apart,
We're not complete, my love.

So, you'll have fun
And I'll have fun,
In each our special way,
Knowing that, when you return,
T'will be a sparkling day.

After the Storm

The wind has abated.
My heart is elated.
Not a leaf is stirring.
My kitty is purring.
All is quiet again.

Nighttime

When I slip into his arms at night,
I feel like a small ship
Dropping anchor in a safe cove.

* * *

As we lie sleeping sweetly together,
Our love enfolds us
Like a rainbow cloud.

* * *

We fall asleep nestled
In the safety of love
And awake to the dawn
Of its passion.

Slipping Into Bed Late

Your sleeping body warms me
As the sunshine warms the fields,
And your circling arms enfold me
In our little world of love.

Changing Values

When is the time
For looking one's best?

Why, home with one's husband —
What matters the rest!

Opening of the Deer-Hunting Season

I'll not be lonely, darling,
While you are far away
For that which is between us
Will keep my spirit gay.

The fire is banked, but the embers glow
And the warmth will still remain
To stir, and flicker, and burst into flame
When you come home again.

The Seasons

Dewdrops sparkle on each golden leaf,
But autumn-time is ever brief.
So enjoy each precious day;
Father Winter's on his way.

* * *

Summertime is far too short
To turn up your nose at the cold.
Winter can be beautiful
Even though the North wind is bold.

You'll have a fire to warm you,
And your husband's close embrace.
You'll have a snug and cozy home
And no cruel winds to face.

So, give thanks to the winter
And the cloudy drifts of snow,
As pure white as an angel's wing,
And the firelight's rosy glow.

We need the cold of winter
To welcome back the spring,
The crocus breaking through the snow
And the songbirds on the wing.

The icy frost will seal the soil
And shield the sleeping plants
Til it's time to break through the earth again
And join the Springtime Dance.

Titles

You are my Prince of Pleasure,
My Duke of Delight,
The Sun of my Day
And the Moon of my Night,
But the finest titles
In all of my life
Are yours, as my Husband
And mine, as your Wife.

Waterfall

When the Current of Life
Which is You
Meets the Current of Life
Which is Me,
Together we tumble
Right over the rim
In joyful unity.

Procrastination
A SONG

Don't put off til tomorrow
What you could do this very day.
You could start this moment
And get it right out of the way.
Hey!

Don't postpone til the next time
When here might be the way
To perform that dreaded task
And make this a Red Letter Day.
Olé!

So I —
Postponed procrastination
Til another day.
I paid all the bills
And balanced the book
And there's still money left
For play.
Hooray!

The Green and the Blue
(A SONG IN ¾ TIME)

You are the green of the Earth
While I am the blue of the Sky.
You are putting down roots
While I am learning to fly.

Some day our contours will blend
In an entity precious and rare
Where I am the green of growing
And you are the blue of the air.

To Duncan —
Happy Valentine's Day

That I love you is something
That is without doubt
For you are someone
Whom I can't live without.

Isn't it lucky
You happen to be
Feeling the very
Same way about me!

Us

I am chilly, you are hot.
I love poetry, you do not.
But on one thing we agree —
Together we're something
We call WE!

Escape Aboard the Lady Beth

The sea is blue and the western sky pink
And gold and orange while clouds, black as ink,
Loom above us, port side and abaft,
As we flee from the storm in our snug little craft.

Lament for Summer

A robin on a leafy bough
Has only thoughts of Here and Now.
He has forgot that sunny hours
Must soon give way to wintry showers,
That flower must fade and petal fall
And joys depart beyond recall.

Dream, Vision, Memory?

I found myself in a forest which extended as far as the eye could see. I don't know in what form I existed, only that I was alive and conscious. Maybe I had no form.

I was in a place of long, long ago, before man existed on this planet, even before there was bird or beast — only the plants in an endless forest, the trees, the sky, the freshest of air and the light.

In a strange way, I was conscious of the roundness of the Earth, that it curved beneath me, that the Forest was everywhere, around and below, and that the sky was endless, beneath and above, and I was rejoicing in being alive.

Whatever it was, it was a strange and profound experience which I will never forget.

To Duncan from Elsie
On Our
Third Wedding Anniversary

December 16, 1991

The sunshine of our love
Will ever beam on high.
No matter what may happen,
It will never leave the sky.

If darkling clouds should dim its glow
Or bitter winds blow by,
The sunshine of our love will ever
Lighten up our sky.

Happiness

My spirit is dancing
Though my feet are standing still.
My spirit is prancing
Right over the hill
Where no one can find it
Or bring it to earth.
My spirit is dancing,
Celebrating its birth.
With arms high in the air
It twirls round and around,
So dance on, little sprite
With one toe on the ground!

(It had not much longer to dance.)

DURING

Intensive Care Unit
February 18, 1993
Condition Critical

Outlook "Not good" (The Doctor)

I would not leave him ever
Because we belong together,
But he is — leaving — me.

The sun is rising
On a new day
And my beloved
Is going away.
God bless him and comfort him
While we are apart.
But, wherever he goes,
He is bearing my heart.

Part of You

Although you cannot speak, my darling,
I can hear your heart.
It tells me that you love me,
That we cannot be apart.
For part of you is part of me
And I am part of you,
And the love we share between us
Will always see us through.

Love Song

My heart is always singing
A love song,
Whether it be one
Of joy or pain.
My heart is always singing
A love song
To tell you that I love you,
Once again.

The next time I called the hospital to inquire about Duncan's condition, I was told "Satisfactory", so I wrote the following little poem of happiness. But, alas, when I reached his room, his condition was still "Critical". "Satisfactory" merely meant it was no worse, I was told.

I.C.U. "Condition Satisfactory"

A vicious wild beast
Held my darling in its grasp,
But he hit it in the ribs
And kicked it in the ass.

Now my beloved
Is "gravely ill" no more,
For he grabbed it by the horns
And threw it out the door!

March

They tell me that it's springtime,
But I see nothing there.
The landscape is snow-covered
And the leafless trees stand bare.

If you look a little closer,
There are signs that can be found,
So, put on your warmest jacket
And go out and look around.

I opened wide the door and found
I had not far to go.
I saw some snow-white snowdrops
Blooming in the very snow.

Their courage and their beauty
Touched my faltering human heart
And spring and hope bloomed once again,
Of my life a part.

The Hurricane

If Seemed As If:

A hurricane came and leveled the house
Where we lived so happily together.
But we're building a new house, starting today,
To withstand the worst of weather.
Board by board, and brick by brick,
We will build it, day by day,
With some of the old and some things quite new,
And mortar to make it stay.
T'will have strength to weather the fiercest gale
And beauty that will last.
We will build for the Future and live in the Now
And treasure our precious Past.

The following poem, "The Climb", is my favorite among those written during this sad time because, in describing Duncan's hoped-for climb back to health, which appeared to be progressing, I was likening it to his much-enjoyed adventures in the woods. He was highly regarded among his hunting pals, in spite of, or maybe because of, his being by far the eldest in his group — in his eighties. They would affectionately decry his habit of using his rifle as a walking stick in difficult places or even while crossing a stream. He would sometimes take little naps while waiting for game to appear. He told me more than once of the pleasure he had relaxing under a tree while watching the antics of an occasional little mouse. And that is why this scene of the woods entered my mind.

The Climb

Duncan is getting better,
Bit by bit each day.
His small smile seems to tell his friends
"I'm coming back to stay.
I know t'will be a struggle,
An uphill climb, at best,
But, as if I were in the woods,
I'll climb, and then I'll rest.

My gun will be my sturdy staff,
And the clasp of my hand is strong,
So I'll grab that big root up above
To help me get along.
A few more footsteps upward,
Although the way is steep,
And now I think I'll settle down
And have a little sleep.

As I sat on the narrow, curving ledge,
Before proceeding on,
A little mouse came out to see
What was going on.

He sat up on his hind legs
And looked, unafraid, at me.
He twinkled his whiskers
And wrinkled his nose
Before frisking by my knee.

The air up here is brisk and fresh
And the mountain view is grand.
And, now that I can see the top,
This is no time to stand!

So I'll climb right up
To the top of the hill,
Where my friends are waiting for me,
And we'll look at the sky
And the woods all around
As far as the eye can see."

The Nursing Home

When Duncan was being moved to the nursing home, LiLi and I followed the ambulance. When we arrived, I went to the desk to speak to the doctor in charge of the floor. He told me, in a matter-of-fact tone, that Duncan had no chance of survival. These words had never been said to me before, and I still had hope. It seemed as if life drained out of me, and I folded in a heap on the floor. Two nurses lifted me into a wheelchair and rolled me after him. And the last phase had begun.

There Comes a Time

When you are dealt
The Cards of Life,
You may discard some
And replace them with others.
But there comes a time
When you must play
Your hand.

Prayer

I pray that my darling may take off soon
For the next world. This is no life for him!
I pray that his passage be peaceful,
Without pain or fear;
That he move toward the Light
And find the new world wonderful;
That he feel safe and at peace
And that the bond between us
Be never broken.
That is my prayer.

To Duncan

If your spirit is tired and wants to go home,
There is nothing for you to fear.
You will find your family in that golden land
And friends whom you hold dear.

Don't worry about leaving me
For your love will keep me strong,
And I'll have a few more things to do
Before I go along.

I'll meet you there, I promise you,
On that you can depend,
My love, my pal, my darling,
My husband, my dearest friend.

A Sad Spring

Apple blossom petals
Float gently to the ground,
As the hours of Life
Slip silently away.

The Sun of Life

Death is a pathway,
Death is a door,
Death is an entrance
To Life Evermore

~And~

Just remember
This, my friend:
Death is a Beginning
It is not an end

~And~

The sun that is setting
From your sky above
Is now also rising
For the one that you love.

SINCE

The Falling Tree: A Dream

Duncan and I were standing in a small clearing in the woods. We were watching a mighty fir tree fall. It trembled and shook and then, as if in slow motion, it toppled slowly to the ground. We watched it with great grief, but the odd and comforting part is that, as we watched it falling, Duncan was standing, whole and unhurt, by my side.

Think of Him

Think of him not
As someone to mourn for.
Think of him rather
As joyful and free,
Exploring God's country
While never forgetting
The ones left behind here,
Like you and like me.

Smiling and laughing
To find himself living,
He is as alive now
As are you and I,
With new perception
And new understanding,
Knowing, at last,
That he never will die.

Letter to My Husband
in Another World

I know that you love me
And keep me in sight
As you follow the path
Of Celestial Light.

You are gaining new knowledge
In your travels on high,
But still keep me in view
From the tail of your eye.

You know more about me, now,
Than I do about you,
So guide me on my passage through
The perils and problems
Of this earthly life.

    Love from

        Your ever-loving wife,

        Elsie

August 1993

My dearest, my darling,
The prince of my heart,
You are guiding me, helping me
Make a new start.
I feel you near me,
Easing the pain
And giving me your strength
Again and again.

Re-union

How can I describe the most wonderful experience of my life? It was beyond anything that I had imagined, anything that I had hoped or prayed for.

I was sitting on the bed with my feet on the floor, wide awake and thinking of Duncan, when suddenly I saw him!

He was sitting as though in a comfortable chair, up where wall and ceiling meet, looking relaxed and peaceful. As our eyes met, I surged out of my body, as if borne on a powerful wave, into his outstretched arms. He held me tightly and we embraced and kissed, and the previous joys we had known paled before this pause in time — he in one world, and I in another, allowed to hold each other for one long, precious moment.

We shouted for joy and kissed each other again, and I found myself back in my body, sitting on the bed. I held my arms up high and cried out, "Thank You. Thank You. Thank You!!!"

Our Love Has Overcome

Our love has overcome
Each separation,
Each obstacle that lay
Across our path,
Each mountain, precipice,
Fast-flowing river,
Til we were in each other's
Arms at last.

My Gallant Knight

My hero, my darling,
My shining knight,
You fought through the shadows
Into the light.
You lifted me up
To the realms of delight,
Filling my lonely heart,
Stilling my fright,
My darling, my hero,
My gallant knight.

My Love Is Alive

My love is alive,
Lively and living,
My love is alive
And I'm in love with you.

I fell in love
With the man that you were.
Now I'm in love
With the spirit you are.

My love is alive,
Lively and living.
My love is alive,
I'm still in love with you.

Now That I Know

Now that you're not
Lying helpless before me,
Now that I know
Your soul's joyful and free,
I will be able
To turn my attention
To other things, knowing
You're still there for me.

(It was not to be that easy.)

One Way, Looking Back

The signs all stated,
The arrows all pointed,
The current flowed deeply
Just One Way.

A fair wind carried us,
Though stray squalls harried us,
Our life-flow bore us
Together — One Way.

After You Left

When you departed, life ground to a standstill.
Nothing here mattered to me anymore,
Whether the sun shone, whether the birds sang,
To Life itself, life had bolted the door.

I did alone things we once did together.
I thought special thoughts without you here to tell.
I walked along paths we once traveled together.
Our little Heaven had turned into Hell.

Then your spirit appeared, alive and rejoicing,
Crying out words only heard by the soul,
"I'm alive! I am well! And I'm once again whole!

"Do not grieve for me, darling, for I am happy.
And one day we'll be together again,
When you have completed the task you were
                              meant for,
Bringing words of comfort to others in pain."

A Perfect Heart

Our love has created
A perfect heart
Of which we both
Are now a part.

So, though you are There
And I am Here,
We can never be sundered,
My dearest dear.

Farewell to Bayville

What happens to Eve
When Adam leaves
The Garden?
Should she walk alone
Remembered paths of love?
Or should she open wide
The golden gates of Eden
And venture forth, with trust
In God Above?

Wherever I Roam

Wherever I wander,
That's where you may find me.
Just wish for me, darling,
And you'll find me there.
And I'll be attracted
As steel to a magnet,
As a lone homing pigeon
Heads straight for its home.

As a frail butterfly
Will fly over the ocean
To its set destination,
I'll fly to you,
For you are my fixed star,
My predestination,
And we'll find each other
Wherever I roam.

Flight of the White Stallion

As I sat on the bed
In a Mexican inn,
An astonishing sight
Came into view:

A great snow-covered mountain
Loomed up before me.
(I was wide awake,
Not wrapped in a dream!)

As, in surprise,
I gazed at the mountain,
I observed a disturbance
On its sloping side.

I looked closer to see
What caused the commotion —
'Twas a great white stallion,
Entrapped in the snow!

His shapely hooves waved
In the air as he struggled
To escape his confinement
In the treacherous snow.

As I watched, spellbound,
From my seat on the daybed,
A small voice within me
Spoke to me and said:

"That horse is Duncan.
It is your beloved."
I held my breath, waiting
For what was to come.

With a final great lurch,
The horse broke from his prison
And, with one leap, landed
On the slim ledge below.

Blue shadows molding
His strong, muscled body,
He gave a great shudder
To shake off the snow.
Then he launched at full gallop —
Off on his way!

When he reached the curve
Where the pathway
Turned leftward,
He did not turn with it
But surged straight ahead.

Off the cold mountainside
Into the sunshine,
Up toward the Unknown
The great stallion soared.

White mane and tail streaming
In the blue all around him,
He diminished in size,
To my sight, as he flew.

Til he seemed no larger
Than a quarter — a nickel —
A dime — a white speck —
And then — he was gone!

I thanked God for bestowing
This beautiful symbol
Of my love's safe departure
Into the Next World.

The Ladder

I am climbing the Ladder of Life.
You will meet me at the top.
I am not afraid of falling.
I know I cannot drop.

With your spirit nearby me,
Happen what may,
I will climb a bit higher
Every day.

I saw doubt and confusion,
Looking back at the past,
But I also saw beauty
And love that will last.

So I'm on my way, darling,
And I will not stop
Til you reach out to help me
Cross the rung at the top.

And we'll be together
Once more, you and I,
Where I won't need a ladder —
I'll know how to fly!

Moments of Sadness

I am hungry,
But there is no food.
I am thirsty,
But the water's not good.
I am lonely.
I miss you so, dear,
I want you only,
But — you are not here.

* * *

Through pain we learn,
Through pain we earn
The Ultimate Joy.

You Are There, Dear God

In the water's fall,
You are there,
In the seabird's call,
You are there.
In the rich, dark loam,
In the tumbling foam,
You are there, dear God,
You are there.

When my heart is glad,
You are there.
When my soul is sad,
You are there.
When I'm all alone
And far from home,
You are there, dear God,
Always there.

Maui

I am enjoying my Self,
For my Self has much to tell me.
I am enjoying my Self,
For my Self has much to say of —

Scenes from the Past
And dreams of the Future,
And the Present, itself
To savor each day
In this land of great beauty,
God's earthly kingdom
Of warm, friendly people
And sparkling blue sea;
Isle of green rolling meadows
And calm grazing horses,
Of peach and gold sunsets
And star-spangled nights;
Where the fragrance of jasmine
Is softly blended
With the dampness of earth
And the freshness of sea;

Where raindrops seek sunbeams
To create a rainbow,
Where waters meet waters
To make waterfalls,
Where mourning doves glide
And butterflies flutter,
Land of towering mountains
And flowering trees.

I am enjoying my daughter,
My comrade and my sister.
Our lives flow like two currents
Side by side in Life's great stream.

The Pool of Tears

A pool of crystal tears stands in my background and is always there. When first it was formed, a violent wind heaved it, and it surged into waves.

It has settled now, but a combination of words, a cluster of beautiful notes, an unexpected memory will cause wavelets of tears to ripple across the surface.

* * *

That is all right. That is good. There is no need to wish the Pool of Tears to be empty. It is part of your landscape, part of your being. The painful sobbing is a thing of the past. The streams of tears are shed. The pool is now at peace. But it will always be there until you two are together again.

Promised Land

Hell is very beneficial
To your growing soul.
So keep that thought in mind, my dear,
Until you reach your goal.

Anyway, there is no Hell.
But there is a Vale of Sorrow,
And that's what you are traveling through
Until you reach Tomorrow.

So keep your spirits high, my dear.
Some day you two together
Will smile as you look back upon
This dark and dismal weather.

You'll walk again in sunshine
Together, hand in hand.
And four blue eyes will sparkle
As you reach your Promised Land.

Our Love is a Beacon

Our love is a beacon
That shines through the darkest night.
All I need to stay on my course
Is to follow its constant light.

So, with my life enriched
By the happiness we knew,
I'll travel along life's pathway
Til I'm once again with you.

Remembering
(Years Later on Maui's Green Shores)

The first time our lips touched,
Two flames burst into being
And, for a breathless moment,
Became one.
And life has never been
The same again, for us.

Insights

Your features on the photograph are fading, but they are engraved on my heart.

* * *

Let not the density of your grief blind your eyes, but open them, rather, to the wonders of life.

* * *

Do not let unimportant things disturb the rhythm of your walk.

There is a spring bubbling in my heart, a spring from an Eternal Source. Sometimes I can catch one of the bubbles. I can crystallize it, and love it, and keep it. But most of the bubbles float away before I can capture them. Never mind, more bubbles will come.

* * *

May the spark
In your heart
Which is God
Become so radiant
That it illumine
Your whole world.

Thanks for the World We Live In

Thanks for the round, diversified World
You have given us for our home.
Thanks for the fields and the marshland
And the rich and fertile loam
Which brings forth the fruit and the flowers,
The lettuce, the carrot, the corn
That feed all the people upon it,
Young, old and newly born.

Thanks for the desert and jungle,
For the camel, the tiger, the bear,
And all the wonderful creatures
Which have their habitat there.

Thanks for the special animals
Which our hearts hold dear,
The dog, the cat and the noble horse,
Our pals throughout the year.

Thanks for the mighty, magnificent sea,
For the fish, the dolphin, the whale,
For the dauntless birds that fly in the sky
As they dip and soar and sail;
For the moon, the stars and the twilight,
For the sun that shines above,
But, most of all, we thank Thee, Lord,
For the priceless gift of Love.

A TOUCH OF HUMOR HELPS
A SORROWING HEART TO HEAL

Now

My memory's small,
My forget-ery's bigger.
I may be vague
But, I've still got my figger!

A Disappointed Friend:

I am having a bit of discouragement
And don't want any more;
For every time I think I'm THERE,
I read: TRY THE OTHER DOOR!

Bare Bottoms on the Beach
(The Thong Bathing Suit)

She is thinking:
"You might like to have
A chat with your friend,
But his eyes keep wandering
To that girl's other end.
Bare bottoms are fine
When they stay in their place —
They belong in the bedroom,
Not waved in your face!"

He is thinking:
"White sails on the ocean,
Bare butts on the beach,
Temptingly lying
Just out of reach,
But there is one trouble
With that sort of thing —
If you see it too much,
It don't mean a thing!"

Entr'acte

Let go of the pain
And remember the romance.
Let go of the grief
And remember the fun.

You must realize
That the story's not over.
The curtain has risen
And a new act begun.

Enchanted Evening in the Forest:
A Precious Memory

A bubbling rill
Behind a hill,
Some mossy stone foundations,
You thought they were
An ancient mill,
Forgot by generations.

As in a dream,
The limpid stream
Of rippling waters ran
O'er rounded stones.
We were alone
As when the world began.

A small green frog
Leapt off a log
With a tiny splash of sound.
An eerie stand of Indian pipes*
Rose, ghostly, from the ground.

*Species of fungus

The pines had shed
A downy bed.
The river sang behind us.
The stars were lace
Behind your face
And love was there
To bind us.

Worlds Within Worlds

The bonds that bind us together
Were forged by joy and pain.
Their strands were interwoven
By heart and soul and brain.
They are made of precious moments
We have shared over the years,
Of work and play and adventure,
Of laughter and of tears —

Hunting for rocks in the countryside,
In woods and abandoned mines,
Our travels took us far and wide
Among birch and towering pines,
Along trickling brooks in the forest
And placid mirrored lakes
Whose marshy banks were a-clatter
With the chatter of ducks and drakes.

We have sailed afar in a gallant ship.
I can see you at the wheel,
In your old straw hat and
                    a pipe in your mouth,
Spume flying along the keel,
Splashing our faces and
                    sprinkling our hair,
Making us laugh. What a happy pair!

We have shared the joys
                    of the Mineral World
And the Animals we held dear.
We have nurtured our garden Flowers
And your orchids "without peer"!
We have adored the sunshine
And the stars in the Sky above
And all these wonders were magnified
When we entered the World of Love.

Depth of Love

The depth of love is measured
By the pain of loss.
So honor the pain
And, slowly, let it go.
Love will remain.

Evil Creatures

One evening I was sitting on my bed when suddenly, four evil, grinning creatures appeared, spaced out in a curve, before and slightly above me. To my surprise, my spirit flew right out of my body, and confronted them.

I flew right up to the first one and, ethereal hands on hips, looked it right in the eye and said, "I'm not afraid of <u>you</u>!" The creature vanished!

I flew up before the second one and the same thing occurred!

When all four evil creatures had been dispelled, I found myself back on the edge of the bed, feeling strong and confident, and full of well-being.

Two Rivers

Two rivers rippled gently through the woods and meadows of Life until, one day, their currents met and they fell and tumbled joyfully over the rim.

The air rang with the music of the love songs they sang as their energies mingled into a rushing stream, and they flowed in oneness together in search of the sea.

5:15 am

No sign of light
Yet in sight,
I lie in the dark, sweet shelter
Of night,
Dreaming of you.

Writing a Poem

In the dark of the night,
I asked myself a question —
"What do you seek
When you're writing a poem?"

I seek rhythm and color
And the right words to conjure
Beauty before us
To gladden our hearts,
That may bring forth a tear
As we summon a sadness;
A smile or a laugh
As we celebrate fun;
To create a poem
Which will capture a picture
And keep it shining
For ages to come.

The Snail

"I go slow,"
Said Madame Escargot.
"But, oh, my friend,
I get there in the end!"

* * *

Meditation on the Sun Deck

My face is in the sun
And the wind is in my hair.
My feet are on the ground
And my spirit's in the air,
Without thought, without emotion,
Without boundary, without care.

Reverie by the Sea

My spirit's confined
To my earthly body
While you, love, are free
As the evening breeze.

You now know secrets
I can only ponder,
As my thoughts wander
By the rippling blue sea.

Moonlight Reverie

Let yourself be
Where river meets sea.
Float like a leaf
On the outgoing tide,
Held in the gentle
Swell of the ocean,
Drifting along
'Neath a calm evening sky.

A pale moon is rising
O'er the darkening waters,
Casting a shimmering
Pathway below.
If you will let yourself
Drift where it takes you,
You will enter the land
Where longings come true.

Another Dimension

When I gaze into the pale gold eyes of one very special cat, as she lies purring contentedly on my chest, I feel that I am somehow connected with another dimension, on a level which is wonderful but which I am unable to understand.

Moonlight

The rays of the moon
Parted the clouds,
Making a frame
For her beauty.

* * *

The Cloud and the Mountain

A great white cloud
Enfolded the mountain
In the tender embrace of a lover,
Veiling their secrets
From the rest of the world.

Afterglow

The sun has slipped out of sight
In a turquoise-tinted sky,
But its rosy radiance still fills the heavens,
Touching even faraway clouds
With glowing pink.

Even so do the memories of our happiness
Illumine my heart.

The sun will rise again
And just as surely,
You and I will be together
When our tomorrow dawns.

Omens

The omens are good,
The free currents flow.
The answers are YES.
They do not say "no".

So, go with the flow
As you hold your head high.
Ride the crest of the wave
Gazing up at the sky.

Birthdays

1993   Eighty-eight —
           Ain't too late!

1994   Eighty-nine —
           Is mighty fine!

1995   Nine-o's divine-o —
           Bring out the wine-o!

1996   Ninety-one —
           A new chapter's begun
           On the Ladder of Life
           I have reached a new rung.
           In the Pool of Existence
           A new pebble's been flung.
           And I am watching the ripples.

1997   Ninety-two —
           All things seem new.
           I have now
           A grander view,
           For the Eye of Wonder
           Is open.

1998   Ninety-three —
And my spirit is free
To fly unencumbered
By triviality.
Seeking the Truth
And releasing the False,
My spirit is dancing
Life's wonderful waltz.

1999   Ninety-four —
My eyesight's getting dimmer
And my hearing's getting fainter,
But my spirit's getting stronger
Than ever before.
For it knows a secret
Which mind can but ponder
Until it is time
To open the door.

2000   Ninety-five —
Glad to be alive
And busy as a bee in a hive,
Collecting my memories
For you to peruse.
That they bring pain or joy
Is for you to choose.

Once Again

Duncan, my beloved,
Is no longer in this world
And the flag of our togetherness
Is, for this lifetime, furled.

But one day I will ride
On Time's outgoing tide,
And we will walk together
Once again, side by side.

The Circle of Life

Life is very tricky,
For how are we to guess
That, if we travel far enough East,
We end up in the West!

But, if you keep on traveling,
Learning as you do,
You'll find, when you reach
Where you started from,
That you are a greater You.

True Gold

I weigh things in
The scales I hold.
I throw out the trash
And treasure the gold.
There is far more gold
Than the eye can see,
I give out love
And love comes back to me.

To You, Dear Reader, Bon Voyage!

May fair winds blow
And the craft that bears you be sturdy.
May your dreams come true
And reality be greater than the dream.

Elsita

The End

But there is no end,
Only new beginnings…

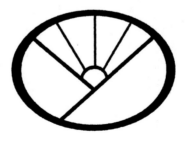

Index